ROCKFORD PUBLIC LIBRARY

3 1112 017817269

 **W9-BIA-742**

WITHDRAWN

J 363.728 MIN
Minden, Cecilia
Reduce, reuse, and recycle

072110

Children's Catalog

ROCKFORD PUBLIC LIBRARY

Rockford, Illinois

www.rockfordpubliclibrary.org

815-965-9511

REDUCE, REUSE, AND RECYCLE

by Cecilia Minden

CHERRY LAKE PUBLISHING • ANN ARBOR, MICHIGAN

ROCKFORD PUBLIC LIBRARY

Published in the United States of America
by Cherry Lake Publishing
Ann Arbor, Michigan
www.cherrylakepublishing.com

Printed in the United States of America
Corporate Graphics Inc
January 2010
CLSP06

Consultants: Sean Gosiewski, Alliance for Sustainability; Gail Saunders-Smith, associate professor of literacy, Beeghly College of Education, Youngstown State University

Editorial direction: Book design and illustration:
Amy Van Zee   Kazuko Collins

Photo credits: Kharidehal Abhirama Ashwin/Shutterstock Images, cover, 1; Shutterstock Images, 5, 9, 22; Dmitrijs Dmitrijevs/Shutterstock Images, 7; Don Bayley/iStockphoto, 10; Margoe Edwards/Shutterstock Images, 13; Dan Moore/iStockphoto, 15; Cindy Hughes/Shutterstock Images, 17; Gurinder Osan/AP Images, 18; Stephanie DeLay/iStockphoto, 20; Becky Hayes/Shutterstock Images, 25; Stephen Finn/Shutterstock Images, 27

Library of Congress Cataloging-in-Publication Data
Minden, Cecilia.
  Save the planet : reduce, reuse, and recycle / by Cecilia Minden.
      p. cm. — (Language arts explorer)
  Includes index.
  ISBN 978-1-60279-662-1 (hardback) — ISBN 978-1-60279-671-3 (pbk.)
 1. Waste minimization. 2. Conservation of natural resources. 3. Recycling (Waste, etc.) I. Title. II. Series.

  TD793.9.M56 2010
  363.72'8—dc22

                                      2009038098

Cherry Lake Publishing would like to acknowledge the work of The Partnership for 21st Century Skills. Please visit www.21centuryskills.org for more information.

TABLE OF CONTENTS

You are being given a mission. The facts in What You Know will help you accomplish it. Remember What You Know while you are reading the story. The story will help you answer the questions at the end of the book. Have fun on this adventure!

Your mission is to learn ways to reduce, reuse, and recycle. Everything you do has an impact on the planet. Every living thing on Earth needs air, water, and materials to survive. As humans use up these resources, we leave behind our ecological footprint. This is the impact of human activities on Earth. What resources will be there for our future?

Let's say you saved your money for months to buy something special. You would want it to last a long time. Wouldn't you take good care of it? Taking care of what we have is often called sustainability. Sustainability means meeting our present needs, but also making sure future generations will be able to meet their needs, too. We have only one Earth. We want it to last a long time. To do this, we must decrease our ecological footprint.

What did you do with the packaging that came with your special purchase? Did you throw it away? Where did it go? How does the trash you create become part of your ecological footprint?

Our field teams are working on ways to reduce trash. Join them as they explore how to reduce, reuse, and recycle. Remember to use What You Know to help you accomplish your mission.

Humans generate a lot of trash.

WHAT YOU KNOW

★ There are almost 7 billion people living on Earth.

★ Most people create trash every day.

★ We are creating trash faster than we are able to find places to put it.

★ Most trash stays with us for thousands of years.

★ People are trying to find ways to reduce, reuse, and recycle products.

Are you ready for news from the field? Here are reports from people who are working on ways to reduce, reuse, and recycle.

For our first stop, we met the field team at Roppongi Hills in Tokyo, Japan. It is one of the world's largest shopping centers. Millions of people visit every year to buy new things. Think about the shopping malls near you. Think of the stores and the products all over the world. What happens to those products? Some of them are still being used. However, many of them have lost their usefulness. They have been thrown away, and new products have been purchased to replace them. This cycle of buying is called consumerism. We buy things, we use them, and we throw away what we don't want. Then we buy more and start all over again. All this creates a lot of trash.

Creating Less Trash

Reducing is one of the easiest ways to decrease our ecological footprint. Simply buy less, use less, and create less trash. The first step is learning to buy only what you need. Check your room. Be sure you don't already have something you can use before buying something new. This can help you save money!

At the mall, our field team observed a shopper reading a list. One of the team members asked her about her

Consumers do not always think carefully about their decisions to purchase items.

shopping. She informed the team that she always makes a shopping list before she goes to a store. She also takes her time looking for exactly what she needs. The list helps her stay focused. She enjoys looking at many items, but she knows she doesn't need to buy them all. She says she wants to learn to be happy with what she already has. If she doesn't find what she needs, then she waits.

After talking to the woman, our team was hungry. We stopped for a snack at the food court. We saw everyone using paper cups, napkins, and straws. A mall worker was taking away many bags of garbage. We wondered where it went. We decided to take only what we needed and use it carefully. That way, we could reduce the amount of trash we created.

PACKAGING

Think about packaging when you shop. For every $11 you spend, $1 is for the packaging. One-third of all trash in the United States is packaging. Some keeps products safe. Most, however, tempts you to buy the product and is not necessary. Look for products with little or no packaging. Look for packaging that can be recycled. Many used items have little or no packaging.

Next, we went into a bookstore. The store had many books, magazines, CDs, and DVDs for sale. Many of the CDs and DVDs were available to rent. Renting is one way to reduce your purchases. Instead of buying a movie, you can rent it, watch it, and then return it. That way, another person can use the item, too! Trading is another way to reduce. Perhaps you and a friend can exchange things, such as clothes or books, rather than buy new ones. Reducing your consumerism will go a long way to decreasing your ecological footprint. ★

Instead of buying a new book, try visiting a used book store to find what you need.

According to the U.S. Environmental Protection
Agency (EPA), each person in the United States creates
4.6 pounds (2.1 kg) of trash every day. That is a lot of
waste! We can discover ways to reduce trash while we shop.
Let's follow our team around a supermarket in Colorado.

The extra packaging on food products often becomes waste.

Smart Shopping

At the store, we saw many items that are disposable. They are meant to be used a few times, and then thrown away. Items such as disposable cameras, razor blades, and paper napkins all have limited use. People purchase them because they are cheap and easy to use. Do you buy paper plates and plastic forks for picnics rather than things you need to wash? These things may be convenient. But how much are we really saving when you add in the cost of hauling the trash away?

Other single-use items are individual packages of food. Puddings, chips, and drinks are handy for lunches. At the supermarket, we met a man who was buying a large jar of applesauce. He explained to us that he splits the servings himself. This way, he doesn't have to pay for extra packaging. He said it takes only a few moments to pack up small portions in reusable containers.

There are more ways to save money and reduce trash. Think about using a permanent water bottle instead of a plastic one. Or, try a lunch box instead of a paper bag. Rethink using paper towels and napkins. Cloth towels and napkins can be washed and used again. Not only are you reducing trash, you are saving money!

As we leave our shopping field site, consider this final way to reduce. Purchase items with durability. Look for products that are well made and repairable. You might pay a little more, but they will last longer. Sometimes we need an item for a short while. Consider renting or borrowing it. Perhaps you and a friend could split the cost and then share the item. ★

PLASTIC BAGS

Some U.S. cities are making plans to put a tax on plastic and paper bags. The cities hope the charge will encourage people to use reusable cloth shopping bags. The money from the tax would be used to clean up areas in the city. However, companies that make plastic and paper bags are fighting back. They say the tax would hurt their businesses. This means it would hurt the people who work for them. What do you think? Should cities put a tax on plastic and paper bags?

Packing a lunch in reusable containers can cut down on trash.

Next, our field workers visited a demolition company in British Columbia. This company saves used bricks, lumber, siding, and other materials from buildings that have been torn down. Instead of throwing away these materials, they sell them to the public in a warehouse. Consumers often come here for lumber and other building supplies.

Reuse Standards

One of the workers at the demolition company explained to us how they choose items for reuse. The building materials must be solid and sturdy. Anything that is rotted or broken is not saved. Then he told us that we can buy more used goods than just building supplies. Goodwill Stores in the United States and Canada operate in a similar way. They accept goods you are no longer using. Goodwill then sells the goods at very low prices. The money is used to pay for training that helps people get jobs.

Just like the reused building supplies, donated items must be in good condition. Clothes should not be torn or dirty. Wash them before you donate them. Check for tears, missing buttons, or worn spots. Test anything

Yard sales and reuse stores have good-quality used items for sale.

electrical. Make sure it still works. Are you donating toys or games? Are all the parts included? Clean, usable items are welcomed.

Later in the day in British Columbia, our field team stopped at a family's yard sale. The family told us they wanted to clear out what they aren't using. They might even make a little money.

Yard sales can be great places to shop. You can also check a reuse center to find what you are looking for. Before buying something new, check out the gently used items that others are giving away. Many people are now using the Internet to let others know they have things to sell or give away. Ask an adult to help you review some of those Web sites.

REUSE CENTERS

ReDO is a nationwide organization. It promotes reuse on many goods that might have otherwise ended up in a landfill. ReDO works to get materials to those who can use them. Food surplus may go to homeless shelters. Medical supplies from one clinic may be needed at another. Office furniture may go to hospitals. Old computers are used to teach students how to repair them. By reusing items, we save on the energy needed to dispose of unwanted trash.

There are many creative ways to reuse what you already have. An old, clean jar could become a vase for flowers.

You can also reuse items in your home in different ways. Plastic sacks from stores can line your garbage cans. Paper sacks make good book covers. Old clothes can become cleaning rags. Milk cartons make nice bird feeders. You can paint cans bright colors to hold desk items. Check out the library for craft books that show other ways to reuse items. ★

Our next field stop is Nigeria, a country in Africa. There aren't any stores in remote areas here. People are resourceful in creating toys and other items. They reuse what they have to make something new. You can see clever bugs and flowers made from tin cans. Baskets made from plastic telephone wire are colorful as well as useful. Plastic wrappers are woven into purses and rugs.

Our team spoke to a woman in Nigeria. She told us that the people in her village look at things in a special way. Before they throw anything away, they think about how they might reuse that item to create something

These Indian men and women created handbags and rugs out of candy wrappers.

SCRAP EXCHANGE

The Scrap Exchange is a reuse center that accepts fabric and other materials that can be used in sewing and other crafts. Many artists and craftspeople shop reuse centers to find materials for their projects. The next time you need materials for a school project, try visiting a store that exchanges materials. Or, set up your own exchange with your friends!

else. Sometimes, they take the item apart to use it in a different way.

Art from Trash

People in other countries such as India have also reused items in creative ways. Broken glass and china are used in mosaic art. The mosaics become trays, pins, or earrings. Metal is reused for rings and necklaces. Clothing is cut and sewn into squares. The squares become quilts, new clothing, and wall hangings. Many of these items are found in fair-trade stores around the world. Professional artists also reuse materials for paintings and sculptures. They even use materials for furniture and houses.

You can do this same thing. Look through closets, drawers, and desks. Help your family figure out what you no longer use. Sell, donate, or give it away to others who will reuse it. Learn to shop at reuse shops. What others discard may be just what you are looking for! ★

Today, our field experts went to the Roskilde Music Festival in Denmark. This festival makes recycling part of the event. Over 80,000 concertgoers can turn in their trash for money. Many are able to earn enough to pay for their tickets by turning in cups and bottles! Items left behind are collected at the end of the event and donated to homeless shelters. One year they donated 1,600 sleeping bags!

Our team interviewed the festival's director. She told us about what can and cannot be recycled. Most recycling centers accept paper, glass, cans, and plastic. Newspaper, office papers, light cardboard, and magazines are all

Clean plastic bottles and aluminum cans are recyclable.

recyclable. Larger items such as phone books or heavy cardboard boxes can also be recycled. Paper must be clean and dry.

Many glass jars and bottles are recyclable. Broken glass is hard to sort, so be careful when you put it in the bins. Window glass, lightbulbs, and drinking glasses are not recyclable.

Cans and jars must be rinsed out, but you do not need to remove the labels. Soup, sauce, or vegetable cans are all recyclable. So are aluminum soda cans. Even lightly used aluminum foil is recyclable.

All plastic items in the United States are stamped with a recycling code from one to seven. Try to buy items stamped with a one or a two. These are the easiest to recycle. If the number is higher, your recycling program may not accept the item. ★

PRECYCLE

You might know that *pre* is a prefix that means "before." When you precycle, you are thinking about recycling before you buy. Ask yourself questions. Do I really need this item? Can I buy in bulk instead of many smaller boxes? Look at the container. Is it one you can reuse or recycle?

We didn't stay long at our next stop. It was too toxic. We were in Guiyu, China, near the world's largest dump for electronic parts. Materials are dumped before they are sorted. Workers make a little more than $5 a day sorting through all the junk to salvage parts. Being around all the electronics, or e-waste, makes them ill.

This isn't the only such dump. There are others around the world. We live in a society that uses many electronics. We must learn to dispose of them in a way that doesn't hurt our environment. In the United States alone, 70 percent of the toxic waste in our landfills is e-waste.

Electronic waste can contain harmful materials that contaminate soil and water.

GREENSCAPES

The U.S. Environmental Protection Agency's GreenScapes program is another way to reduce our ecological footprint. Land is usually cleared before building. Trees, bushes, and rocks are hauled away or burned. Expensive landscaping is done. This hurts the environment. It is better to include what is already there in the design. Don't cut down the trees. Build the design around them. Don't haul away the rocks. Use them to line the flower beds. GreenScapes offers suggestions for companies that do large-scale landscaping.

Electronics are not the only harmful waste. There are many chemicals from household products and manufacturing plants that create toxic waste. Car parts and construction materials do, too. How can we prevent these toxic materials from harming our environment?

Avoid products that have the words *poison* or *danger* on the label. Avoid buying items that will be difficult to recycle. If you must buy them, recycle responsibly. There are currently 3,000 household hazardous waste (HHW) centers in the United States. These centers accept items such as batteries, household cleaners, and paints. Some of these products can be reused, recycled, or reprocessed. ★

Our final stop was Mount Trashmore Park in Virginia Beach City, Virginia. You might think this is an unusual name for a park. Well, it is a very unusual park. Mount Trashmore was created on top of a landfill.

A landfill is a system of layering trash with dirt to fill in a depressed, or low, area of ground. Think of a sandwich. You start with a slice of bread. Then you add lettuce, cheese, and whatever else you like. You top it with another slice of bread.

This is how Mount Trashmore was built. It began as a landfill. A layer of trash was added, and then a layer of dirt. Then it was topped with grass. Now, there are 165 acres (67 ha) of sports parks, trails, and picnic areas. The park

WASTE TO ENERGY

Not all trash ends up in landfills. Trash is also burned to create energy. Incinerators are huge ovens. Trash is put into the ovens. Water is run through pipes near the ovens. The water gets so hot it becomes steam. The steam fuels heat or generates electricity.

Once a landfill, Mount Trashmore is now a park.

also features the Water Wise Garden. There, you can learn how to plant a great garden with a small amount of water.

We met a woman who worked at the park. She told us about how important it was that the landfill was made of clean items. If items in the trash are harmful, they will seep into the ground around a landfill. They might harm nearby water or spoil crops. The park continues to be watched to make sure nothing from the landfill is toxic to the environment.

Many landfill parks exist around the world. What a cool way to reduce, reuse, and recycle our trash! ★

MISSION ACCOMPLISHED!

Congratulations! You followed our field teams to learn the best ways to reduce, reuse, and recycle. You learned that reducing what we buy also helps reduce trash. You know how to make better choices about receiving and disposing goods. You learned what can be recycled. Congratulations on finishing your mission. Now you can shrink your ecological footprint by reducing, reusing, and recycling.

CONSIDER THIS

Consider other ways you can help reduce trash. By asking yourself more questions about reducing, reusing, and recycling, you might just start a mission of your own!

★ In what ways could a family reduce their consumption of goods?

★ How can reducing waste help our environment? How does reusing items help the environment?

★ Think of three ways you could reuse a glass bottle.

★ Why is sustainability important?

★ How do reducing, reusing, and recycling help the sustainability of the earth?

RECYCLING POINT
This site is provided for the recycling of materials only
Under no circumstances should general waste be disposed of at this site

Food and drinks cans only

WASTE PAPER ON

Some public parks have separate containers for glass, cans, and paper to be recycled.

bulk (BUHLK) a large quantity of something that is not divided into separate packages

consumerism (kuhn-SOO-muh-riz-um) an attitude that leads to buying many things, throwing them away, and then buying more

demolition (de-muh-LI-shuhn) tearing down buildings and other dwellings

disposable (diss-POH-zuh-buhl) created to be used once and then thrown away

durability (dur-uh-BI-li-tee) able to exist for a long time

ecological footprint (ee-kuh-LOG-ih-cul FUT-print) the negative impact of human activities on Earth

landfill (LAND-fil) an area of low-lying land filled with layers of trash and dirt

landscaping (LAND-skay-ping) using plant cover to enhance a space

mosaic (moh-ZAY-ik) artwork made with small pieces of stone or glass

resources (REE-sorss-ez) valuable things found on Earth, such as water and trees

seep (SEEP) to spread slowly

toxic (TOK-sik) harmful to the health of people and the environment

LEARN MORE

BOOKS

Anton, Carrie. *Earth-Smart Crafts: Transform Toss-Away Items into Fun Accessories, Gifts, Room Decor & More!* Middleton, WI: American Girl, 2009.

Hewitt, Sally. *Reduce and Reuse.* New York, NY: Crabtree Publishing Company, 2008.

Knight, M. J. *Why Should I Recycle Garbage?* Collingwood, ON: Saunders, 2009.

WEB SITES

National Institute of Environmental Health Sciences (NIEHS) Kids' Pages

http://kids.niehs.nih.gov/recycle.htm

> Learn more ways you can reduce, reuse, and recycle at this Web site.

Reduce.org

http://reduce.org

> Reduce.org outlines how to reduce waste while traveling, at school, and during the holidays.

The U.S. Environmental Protection Agency

http://www.epa.gov/waste/conserve/rrr/index.htm

> The EPA gives tips and tricks about composting, disposing of hazardous waste, and how to produce less waste.

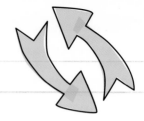

FURTHER MISSIONS

HOW TO ORGANIZE YOUR FAMILY RECYCLING CENTER

Your family can work together to create a recycling center in your home. Begin by checking your town's Web page. What items does your town collect for recycling? There will probably be tips on the Web page for how to prepare items. Be sure materials are clean and dry. Clearly label each container. Make a habit of checking the containers. Is everything in the right box? Many cities pick up these recyclable materials once a week. Make sure you bring your containers to the curb in time for pickup.

CALCULATING YOUR FOOTPRINT

The Global Footprint Network has a calculator to help you find out how big your ecological footprint is. Make this a family project. Go to http://www.footprintnetwork. org/en/index.php/GFN/page/personal_footprint/ and click on the quiz. It will ask you questions about your lifestyle. For example, do you use products that travel from long distances? Then fuel is needed to transport them. Everything you do makes a difference. Check it out and see how your family measures up.

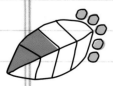

INDEX

ABOUT THE AUTHOR

Cecilia Minden, PhD, is a literacy consultant and author of more than 100 books for children. Cecilia lives with her family in North Carolina. They always reuse, reduce, and recycle!

ABOUT THE CONSULTANTS

Sean Gosiewski is currently the program director of the Alliance for Sustainability in Minneapolis, Minnesota. He has worked with volunteers in neighborhoods, schools, congregations, and local governments to make their homes, organizations, and communities more sustainable.

Gail Saunders-Smith is a former classroom teacher and Reading Recovery teacher leader. Currently she teaches literacy courses at Youngstown State University in Ohio. Gail is the author of many books for children and three professional books for teachers.